Mr Marvel liked to do magic tricks.

His friend, Squeak, the mouse, liked
to help him.

Mr Marvel tried lots of magic tricks
but they always seemed to go wrong.

One day Mr Marvel wanted a car.

'I want a car,' said Mr Marvel.
'I can help you,' said Squeak.

'ABRACADABRA!' said Squeak.
'We want a car.'

'Here is a car,' said Mr Marvel.
'But it is too little.'

'No, it is not too little,'
said Squeak.
'I like it.'

'I can't go in this car,'
said Mr Marvel.
'I am too big.'

'ABRACADABRA!' said Mr Marvel.
'I want a big car!'

'Here is a car,' said Squeak.
'But is it too big?'

'No, it is not too big,'
said Mr Marvel.
'I like it.'

'I will go in the big car,'
said Mr Marvel.

'I will go in the little car,'
said Squeak.

'Here we go!' said Mr Marvel.
'Here we go!' said Squeak.